SEPTEMBER STORM

The German Invasion of Poland

Text by Gordon Rottman
Color plates by Stephen Andrew

Introduction

The 1936-39 Spanish Civil War has often been described as a proving ground for the weapons and tactics of World War II. This is somewhat overstated as only small numbers of weapons seeing World War II service were actually employed in Spain. It was Germany who made the most of this opportunity employing some tanks, aircraft, and other weapons there, albeit on a comparatively small scale. Likewise the tactics employed in Spain only scratched the surface of the coming large-scale Blitzkrieg (lightning war) operations employing massed armor supported by infantry formations, artillery, and aircraft. While Germans of the Condor Legion manning tanks and aircraft gained valuable experience, suggested refinements to their equipment, and practiced some of the tactical concepts that would later be the hallmark of the Blitzkrieg, it was on a limited scale.

Improvements to equipment and refinements to tactics were certainly made based on Spanish Civil War experiences and lessons learned, as they were from ongoing field exercises, testing at research center, and studies and testing conducted by arms manufacturers. Unit organizational concepts and command and control procedures for large formations as well as developing a logistical system capable of sustaining large-scale offensive operations for a prolonged period were improved in the pre-war years. World War I had taught the Germans that in order to win a war, offensive operations would have to be executed swiftly and the main enemy force decisively defeated. Once an initial offensive had bogged down then the possibility of a stalemate developing and turning into a long drawn-out protracted war of attrition. Germany knew it could not win another such war.

The real proving ground for the weapons and tactics Germany would use in the early stages of World War II was not Spain, but Poland. The full weight of the German Army (Heer) and the Air Force (Luftwaffe) would be thrown at Poland to overwhelm one of the larger Eastern European armies in five weeks. The War Navy (Kriegsmarine) played a negligible role and the fledgling SS-Verfügungstruppe (Special Employment Troops—not redesignated the Waffen-SS until 1940) supplemented Army infantry units.

German forces thrown at Poland were organized into two army groups (Heersgruppe), five armies (Armee), 13 army corps (Armeekorps), one motorized corps (motorisiert Korps), an armor corps (Panzerkorps), and two provisional corps controlling 42 infantry (Infanteriedivision), three motorized infantry (Infanteriedivision [motorisiert]), three mountain (Gebirgsdivision), six armor (Panzerdivision), and four light divisions (leichtdivision); several provisional brigades and separate regiments, plus three puppet Slovakian infantry divisions. Germany had mobilized some 700,000 troops backed by almost 3,300 tanks. The Luftwaffe would commit almost 2,100 aircraft.

This massive juggernaut was faced by a well trained, but under-equipped Polish Army heavily reliant on reserve forces. Reserve units were still in the process of mobilizing even into the campaign's last weeks. Prior to the German invasion, the active Polish Army consisted of 500,000 troops in six armies (Poland did not employ a corps echelon), 30 infantry divisions, 11 cavalry brigades, three mountain brigades, and two mechanized brigades. Additional divisions and brigades would be raised from mobilized reserve, National Guard, and Border Defense Corps units. The potential reserve pool included thee million men. Poland had only 388 mostly obsolescent and obsolete operational combat aircraft. Some 950 other aircraft, combat and non-combat, were in storage or reserve, undergoing repairs, or assigned to training units.

The German Blitzkrieg doctrine called for multiple deep penetrations by Panzer and other mobile forces to thrust into the enemy rear areas to destroy combat forces in their path, artillery positions, headquarters, and rear service organizations. Flanks were frequently ignored with emphasis on striking deep and disrupting the enemy's defensive plan, command and control, and lines of communications. Frontline enemy forces would be splinted and often separated into pockets cutoff from retreat or reinforcement to be dealt with by follow-on infantry forces. Other infantry forces would hold by-passed enemy frontline forces in-place with limited attacks. Artillery would support the mobile forces and reconnaissance units would spread out ahead of the mobile forces to seek weakly defended routes or gaps in the line. Pioneers (combat engineers) would follow closely on the heeds of the attack force to breech obstacles and bridge rivers replacing destroyed bridges. Luftwaffe dive-bombers would support the advance serving as an extension to the artillery while fighters destroyed enemy aircraft in the air and on the ground. Medium bombers attacked deeper targets, industrial sites, railroad lines and marshalling yards, troop concentrations, and reserves moving to the front. Another factor that greatly enhanced the ability to accomplish Blitzkrieg tactics was the extensive use of radio communications in a well-developed network.

While the German Army is often thought of as a highly mobile offensive force based on tanks, it was still very much an infantry centric force. Of the 58 divisions committed to Poland only 13 were mobile (six armor, four light, and three motorized infantry divisions). The 45 infantry divisions moved only as fast as their foot-borne infantrymen. While some of their support elements were motorized, the antitank, pioneer and signal troops for example, all the artillery and supply units from division to company-levels were horse-drawn. This also applied to much of the corps and army-level artillery, supply, and service troops. What motorized transport was available was often in short supply, of limited load capacity, and lacked all-wheel-drive, a serious deficiency on Eastern Europe's poor road system.

The Panzer divisions were not as powerful as sometimes imagined. Granted, they did possess sufficient firepower, shock power, and mobility to be decisive, especially against less well trained infantry forces prepared for more static warfare on a linear front and backed by limited and outdated artillery, little if any armor, denuded of what air support they had expected, and themselves relying on horse transport and even fewer trucks.

Most of the German tanks were extremely light and already obsolete or at least obsolescent. They lacked substantial armor protection, possessed only limited cross-country mobility, and obstacle defeating capability. Most were armed with only machine guns and 2cm automatic cannons. Of the over 3,200 German tanks committed to Poland, only 368 were armed with 3.7cm or 7.5cm guns. The Panzer and other mobile divisions' artillery were towed by halftracks and trucks, but they lacked full-tracked self-propelled artillery. Most of their supporting and service units were fully motorized. The four light divisions were basically mechanized cavalry formations with some tanks, light truck and motorcycle-mounted infantry, and motorized artillery and support. None of the infantry battalions assigned to Panzer or other mobile divisions were transported by armored halftracks at this time.

There were other, less critical, deficiencies in German equipment. Later raised divisions possessed fewer trucks and radios. Older model machine guns were substituted for the modern 7.92mm MG34 machine gun, antitank guns were in short supply, and mortars replaced some infantry guns. The fledgling SS-Verfügungstruppen was still developing and largely armed with impounded foreign weapons.

The Polish Army was one of the largest in Eastern Europe, relatively well trained, highly motivated, and professionally led. It was designed to resist border incursions as neighbors attempted to chip away at disputed territories and a traditional invasion on a linear front. Its doctrine and capabilities were inadequate for what it was about to face. In order to defend its territory, almost as large as France, Poland maintained large and well-organized reserves. Poland's equipment was a mix of modern, obsolescent, and obsolete gear. The modern equipment though were few in number and either thinly spread through the army or concentrated in a small number of specialized units. Some of Poland's light tanks, antitank guns, and antiaircraft guns were among the best available, but there were simply not enough of them. One of the main deficiencies with Polish tactics was the same as would be experienced by France in the following year. Its approximately 400 tanks were too widely distributed to be an effective counteroffensive force. Most of the tanks were even less capable than the light German tanks. They were extremely light; many were machine gun-armed tankettes of no offensive use. Others were completely obsolete dating from World War I. Many Polish weapons were obtained from France or license-built designs. Sweden also supplied weapons, as did Czechoslovakia and some German designs were utilized, some of which were obtained after World War I. A very small number of older Russian weapons were used along with some Austrian arms. A small number of native designs were also produced. The Polish Army had few radios and command and control would be severely hampered.

The German invasion plan, Fall Weiss (Case White) was its forces divided into two army groups, North and South. Army Group North (Heeresgruppe Nord) attacked out of northern Germany into the Polish Corridor with 4th Army. Its other army, the 3rd, was positioned in East Prussia and would attack southward toward Warsaw. Heeresgruppe Süd had three armies arrayed from north to south, 8th, 10th and 14th, with part of the latter attacking northward out of Slovakia with three divisions from that puppet state into the thinly held Polish flank. The heaviest concentration of German forces was in the 10th Army. Once the invasion began though these forces would gravitate northward swinging toward Warsaw and to the south overwhelming Krakions

The Polish plan, Plan Z (Zachod—West) saw the bulk of the army positioned along the western frontier, light screening forces on the south facing Slovakia and others scattered along the northern frontier with East Prussia. Substantial reserves were positioned in the interior. Additional reserve units would be mobilized in phases if Germany invaded. The forward named Polish armies were arrayed from north to south: Pomorze, Poznan, Lodz, Kraków, and Karpaty with Army Modlin facing East Prussia. Army Prusy backed Army Lodz and there were three reserve groupings. Army Matopolska would later be sent to the south flank.

The invasion commenced on 1 September 1939 taking the Poles completely by surprise. Regardless of the Germans derisively referring to the campaign as the "Autumn Maneuvers," the Poles gave a good account of themselves in spite of the overwhelming odds. In many instances it was not a rout or walkover as is sometimes assumed. Stiff Polish resistance caused the Germans delays and some setbacks. A week into the campaign the Germans approached Warsaw and fighting there would be vicious and prolonged. The city did not surrender until 27 September after heavy aerial bombardment. On 17 September the Soviets invaded from the east against negligible resistance. Scattered fighting would continue throughout Poland as the Germans and Russians pressed in. The last Polish forces surrendered on 6 October, making it far longer than the "18-day campaign" claimed by German propagandists. In spit of mass surrenders, up to 100,000 Polish troops made it out of Poland into Romania, Hungary, and the Baltic states to later fight on the side of the Allies in other theaters.

The Germans lost some 16,000 dead and 32,000 wounded. Over 670 tanks were knocked out with just over 200 being un-repairable. Almost 200 artillery pieces and mortars were lost along with over 300 armored cars, over 6,000 trucks, and 5,500 motorcycles. Over 280 German aircraft were downed and about the same number seriously damaged. The Soviets lost less than 1,000 troops.

Over 66,000 Polish military were killed and 134,000 wounded. Losses to the Soviets are unknown. The Germans took 587,000 prisoners and the Soviets 200,000. Virtually all Polish aircraft were lost except for 100 escaping to Romania. Most of the small Polish Navy escaped as well.

Germany incorporated much of western Poland into the Reich, 35,000 square miles (90,000 square kilometers). The Soviets seized 77,500 square miles (201,000 square kilometers) of western Poland, which would eventually be seized by Germany. Poland ceased to exist as Germany dissolved all trappings of Polish government, institutions, and culture. A core of south-central Poland remained as the Generalgouvernement (General Government), 37,000 square miles (96,000 square kilometers) as a slave labor pool and envisioned to provide farming land for German "settlers." The liberation of Poland would see extremely vicious fighting and even greater loss of life than in the 1939 campaign. Hundreds of thousands of Poles were employed in forced labor and over six million Poles would die in uprisings, partisan warfare, reprisals, starvation, and extermination during the five-year German occupation and subsequent liberation.

Photograph Credits
Imperial War Museum, Süddeutscher Verlag Bilderdienst, Ullstein, Bundesarchiv, and HITM.

General Field Marshal Walther von Brauchitsch (right), Commander in Chief of the Defense Forces (Oberbefehlshaber des Wehrmacht), and General of Artillery Franz Halder (left), Commander in Chief of the Army (Oberbefehlshaber des Heers), discuss unit movement plans for Fall Weiss (Case White), the Poland invasion plan, in August 1939. The General Staff had collected and analysed a great deal of intelligence information on Poland including aerial photographs, maps, and information reported by agents posing as travelers and businessmen. General Halder wears the older Reichsheer tunic.

Motorized vehicles of a headquarters staff of a signal unit pass a 10.5cm IFH 16 light field howitzer battalion. Many divisional artillery units were armed with this obsolescent weapon rather than the more modern 10.5cm IFH 18. German artillery, supply, and other service troops were mostly horse-drawn. In the foreground appears to be an early Stoewer staff car preceded by a motorcycle and an Opel Olympia sedan, a civilian vehicle widely used as a light staff car. The rectangular symbol with an extension on the side above the staff car's registration plate is the symbol of a signal unit.

To provide a cover for the massive troop build up on the Polish frontier in East Prussia, the explanation was given as the annual autumn maneuvers, a longstanding German traditional, and in this instance it was to commemorate the German victory of Russia during the 1914 Battle of Tannenberg in East Prussia. Here staff offices of Panzerverband Kempf (Armor Formation), commanded by SS-Oberstgruppenführer (equivalent to a general) Werner Kempf, assemble for orders during the August exercise. An umpire is identified by his white cap band. Panzerverband Kempf (aka Panzerverband Ostpreussen or Panzer-Division Kempf) was an ad hoc brigade-sized formation comprised of the 4.Panzer-Brigade as its headquarters, Panzer-Regiment.7, and SS-Standarte "Deutschland" under I.Armeekorps, 3.Armee. An SS-Standarte was an old term for a regiment. The Waffen-SS would later adopt the regiment term.

Troop deployments increased and units moved eastward to concentrate on the Polish border in Pomerania and Silesia, in northern Slovakia, a German protectorate, and in the Free City of Danzig (today's Gdansk) and East Prussia, cut off from Greater Germany by the Polish or Pomerania Corridor. This corridor, defined by Germany proper on the west and East Prussia and Danzig on the east, was Poland's only link to the Baltic Sea. Deployments were phased with the first units moving in mid-June 1939. In some instances deployed units were returned to their home garrisons in order to deceive the Poles on German intensions and later redeployed to the frontier. These troops have been issued shoulder straps devoid of the embroidered unit designation number as a security measure. Additionally, these are old-type straps, which lacked edge piping identifying the arm of service. The two chevrons identify the soldier as an Obergefreiter with less than six years service, an assistant group (squad) leader.

Panzerverband Kempf's maneuvers in East Prussia saw the first instance of a joint German Army and SS-Verfügungstruppe (Special Employment Troops—redesignated Waffen-SS in 1940) unit being formed. The Division would support the 11. and 21.Infanterie-Divisions' 1 September attack on the Mlawa defenses south of East Prussia. The motorcyclist watching SS-Oberstgruppenführer Kempf is SS-Verfügungstruppe, identifiable by his camouflage helmet cover and black shoulder straps (Army straps were dark blue-green.) The wear of the gas mask canister on the chest was standard for motorcyclists and others riding motorized vehicles.

During Panzerverband Kempf's maneuvers SS-Obersturmbannführer (equivalent to a lieutenant colonel) Paul Hausser, Inspector of the SS Leader's School(SS-Junkerschule), accompanied the Panzerverband through the Polish campaign as an observer and would later command the SS-Verfügungsdivision when the various SS regiments (Standarte) were consolidated into a single formation in October. Maps of Poland were issued to commanders anointed with fictitious place names overlaid on actual terrain. Prior to the invasion the fabricated place maps on all maps were converted to actual names, a time consuming and tedious task for staff personnel. Quietly civilians in the border zone were moved out as troop units deployed for the invasion. This was for the sake of the civilians' safety as well as to further maintain security and prevent refugees from interfering with troop movements and supply efforts.

Newly assigned recruits of SS-Standarte "Deutschland," attached to Panzerverband Kempf, swear their oath of allegiance to Führer and Fatherland during maneuvers in East Prussia just prior to the invasion. The original invasion date was set for 25 August 1939, but additional time was required to deploy the five German armies and massive supporting services. It was reset for 0445 hours, 1 September.

1 September 1939

At 0425 hours the first German aircraft launched heading for their targets in Poland. While the invasion was to be commenced at 0445 hours, the first action occurred at 0430 hours as Stuka dive-bombers prematurely struck the Tczen bridge in the Polish Corridor. Here a Heinkel He-111H-3 bomber takes off roaring over the crew of a 4-meter Em.R.4m. rangefinder of an 8.8cm flak battery protecting the airfield. Minutes later Polish observers began reporting waves of German aircraft winging over the border.

The Heinkel He-111H-3 was one of the Luftwaffe's mainline medium bombers along with the Dornier Do-17Z and Junkers Ju-88A-1; a total of 648 medium bombers were unleashed on Poland. The He-111 was armed with three 7.92mm MG.15 machine guns, one in the nose, one in a rear facing dorsal position, and another in a rear facing ventral position. There was a mounting for an additional machine gun on either side in the aft side ports, but these were seldom fitted until the Battle of Britain. Most bombers at this time were painted in a two-tone dark and medium green splinter pattern and a light grey underside. Aircraft identification was in the form of black code letters and numbers on the fuselage sides, the specific aircraft within a squadron (Geschwader) identified by a white (occasionally yellow or black) letter to the viewer's right of the national insignia. This letter was repeated outboard of the national insignia on the left wing, white or yellow on the upper surface and black on the underside.

The Junkers Ju-87B-1 Stuka (contraction of Sturzkampfflugzeug—dive-bomber) developed a fearsome reputation during the Polish Campaign and subsequent operations. Vulnerable to enemy fighters, it soon became obsolete, but remained in use through the war. A total of 219 were committed against Poland. Armament consisted of a 7.92mm MG.17 in each wing and a 7.92mm MG.15 in the rear cockpit. These Stukas, returning from a mission attacking Polish airfields or troops moving to the front, have dropped their payloads, but they typically carried a 500kg (1,100-lb) bomb beneath the fuselage and two 50kg (110-lb) bombs beneath each wing. Stukas were typically painted solid dark green with a light grey underside.

The aircrews of a He-111H-3 unit stand at attention prior to receiving their orders at the Pinnow Airfield. This medium bomber could carry 2,000kg (4,400 lbs) of bombs in an internal bomb bay. Larger bombs could be carried on an external rack beneath the bomb bay. It had a crew of five. In addition to medium and dive-bombers, the Luftwaffe employed 426 Messerschmitt Bf-109 and Bf-110 fighters and almost 500 reconnaissance aircraft, transports, and other aircraft. It even sent in 30 obsolete Henschel Hs-123A-1 bi-wing dive-bombers as close support aircraft. Even some Ju-52 three-engine transports were later employed to drop incendiary bombs over Warsaw.

Bomber pilots study their assigned targets over Warsaw. One of the pilots is an Unteroffizer (corporal). Most bomber pilots were NCOs. Escorted by Bf-110 twin-engine fighters, Warsaw was bombed from 3,000 meters (9,840 feet) by He-111s and Do-17s in the early morning hours of the first day of the Second World War.

The invasion commences under an artillery barrage against known Polish positions along the frontier. Here 10.5cm lFH 18 field howitzers of 3.Batterie, Artillerie-Regiment.20, 20.Infanterie-Division open fire at dawn. The 10.5cm field howitzer was the standard divisional artillery piece, with 36 per division in three battalions. Its range was 9,425 meters. Contrary to the impression left by motion pictures and television, the 8.8cm gun was an antiaircraft gun and was not employed as field artillery, though it was occasionally employed as an ad hoc antitank gun.

A German soldier stands guard on an abandoned camouflaged Polish supply train captured at Kartuzy (Karthaus) on the war's first day. The weapon is an obsolescent French-made 75mm antiaircraft gun, which had seen some action against the Luftwaffe. The guard wears the standard uniform of the period with a field grey (grey-green with the green predominating) tunic with dark blue-green collar and shoulder straps and stone grey trousers. Field grey trousers were more commonly worn though.

A German artillery battery crosses the frontier beside a Polish customs house with its 10.5cm IFH 18 field howitzers followed by an Hf.7 steel field wagon (Stahlfeldwagen). The latter was an all-metal, rubber-tired utility wagon drawn by four houses. Older-style wooden bed, spooked wooden-wheeled wagons and carts were in much wider use though.

German infantrymen and dark blue-uniformed frontier police (armed with older and longer Ger.98 rifles than the standard Kar.98k carbine carried by the infantrymen) force the frontier gate out of the road into Poland from the Free City of Danzig beside the Polish customs house at Gdynia. The gate is red and white striped, the Polish national colors. The infantrymen have fashioned helmet bands from web bread bag carrying straps, though they have not attached camouflaging foliage.

A column of Pz.Kpfw.I light tanks cross a road where stones had been stacked to construct roadside walls. In the center is a Pz.Kpfw.II. Panzerkampfwagen (Pz.Kpfw.) translates simply as armor battle vehicle—a tank. The obsolete Pz.Kpfw.I Ausf.B (Ausf. = Ausführung—variant) was by far the most numerous tank equipping Panzer divisions at the war's beginning. The 5.8-ton tank was armed with only two 7.92mm MG.34 machine guns and crewed by two men. Maximum armor thickness was only 13mm (1/2-inch) and a minimum of 7mm. Its speed was 27 mph with an operating range of 88 miles. They proved to be none too reliable for long distance movements under non-stop combat conditions.

In the foreground are two Pz.Kpfw.II Ausf.A light tanks. Between the two Pz.Kpfw.IIs is a Opel Blitz four-wheel truck and directly above it is a then scarce 3.7cm gun-armed Pz.Kpfw.III (probably an Ausf.B or C—differences were mostly internal) followed by a Pz.Kpfw.II and then an even scarcer 7.5cm gun-armed Pz.Kpfw.IV (probably an Ausf B or C). Another Pz.Kpfw.IV can be seen behind the six-wheel truck. Fewer than 200 Pz.Kpfw.IIIs existed at this time along with barely over 200 Pz.Kpfw.IVs and not all were deployed to Poland. By far the most common tank in the photograph is the Pz.Kpfw.I. The open light car beside the second foreground Pz.Kpfw.II is a Stoewer. As can be seen, even Panzer divisions still relied on draft horses to some degree. This formation is probably from the 10.Armee.

A column of Pz.Kpfw.IIs winds its way toward a railroad embankment underpass tunnel. Interspersed are a few Pz.Kpfw.Is and IVs. There appears to be a light colored cloth panel for air-to-ground identification placed on the engine deck of many tanks. To the left an element of a motorcycle rifle company, led by a Horch staff car.

An 8cm (actually 81mm) sGrW.34 heavy mortar crew has dug into a hasty emplacement. The parapet is camouflaged with grass stalks cut from the surrounding field. A freshly turned parapet is easily detectable from the air. An infantry battalion's machine gun company, besides 12 7.92mm MG.34 heavy machine guns, had a platoon of six 8cm mortars. The 64kg mortar had a 2,400-meter range. Mortars were painted field grey with a white stripe down the top of the barrel as an alternate sighting aid.

Infantry troops of 19.Infanterie-Division wait for the order to move across the Polish frontier as the Luftwaffe and artillery clear the way. These men are reservists outfitted with World War I M16 helmets rather than the current standard M35. Besides an MG.34 machine gun seen to the right, they possess an MG.15, issued as a stopgap substitute, adapted from an aircraft weapon, as there were insufficient MG.34s available. The individuals with a single chevron carry the rank of Gefreiter. An Unteroffizer (corporal—a group [squad] leader), identifiable by the braid-edged shoulder straps and collar can be seen to the center left.

A dispatch rider halts beside a Polish truck destroyed in a Luftwaffe attack. His protective coat is rolled up and attached to his motorcycle along with his mess kit. An M35 dispatch case is slung over his shoulder.

Infantrymen examine a Polish license-built Swedish 3.7cm Bofors wz.36 (wz. = wzór—model) antitank gun captured as they crossed the frontier. This was a better weapon than the German's own 3.7cm PaK.35/36 penetrating 17 percent more armor. They were later impressed into German service as the 3.7cm PaK.36(p). The Poles claimed these guns knocked out up to 150 German tanks and 100 armored cars. Active Polish infantry regiments possessed nine of these excellent weapons while most reserve regiments had only four.

Fighting erupted in Free City of Danzig between local Polish troops and German forces comprised of the militarized Danzig Police, Army infantry units, and SS-Heimwehr Danzig_(Home Defense Danzig). The latter possessed a number of former Austrian Austro-Daimler ADGZ eight-wheel armored cars (the two center axels mounted dual wheels). They were armed with a 2cm KwK.35 gun and a 7.92mm machine gun in the turret, another 7.92mm in the rear hull, and sometimes one in the forward hull. These were distinctively identified by the "SS" runes and death head insignia in white. This scene depicts the hard fighting around the Danzig Post Office, defended by postal workers, in which four of the armored cars participated. Other SS ADGZs fought in Gdynia.

Attacking out of East Prussia Panzerverband Kempf supported the 3.Armee. Here SS-Oberstgruppenführer Kempf's command tank, a Pz.Kpfw.III Ausf.B modified with a frame-type radio antenna mounted on the engine deck, which prevented the turret from being rotated 360 degrees. It appears the bow machine gun has been removed to make room for additional radio equipment. The white Balkenkreuz (beamed cross) was added to all tanks and other combat vehicles just prior to the invasion. Painted on all four sides, unmarked vehicles were considered enemy. The Poles effectively used the distinctive marking as an aiming point. To counter this they were sometimes subdued by smearing mud over them or painting them in the dull yellow used for unit insignia. They were soon ordered removed from the fronts of vehicles and then the others removed. In October it was replaced by the white outlined black Balkenkreuz. The white "B01" on the hull side identifies the command of Panzerverband Kempf, a brigade-sized formation.

A Pz.Kpfw.IV Ausf.B of 10.Panzer-Division rolls though Grudziadz in the Polish Corridor as Volksdeutsch citizens welcome the liberators. The Division, part of the Army Group North's reserve, moved into East Prussia and then attacked into north-central Poland to turn the Polish northern flank. The Pz.Kpfw.IV Ausf.B was armed with a short 7.5cm gun and two 7.92mm MG.34 machine guns, one in the right side of the gun mantel and the other in the right bow.

Troops of Hitler's personal bodyguard, SS-Leibstandarte "Adolf Hitler," await the order to advance against the stubbornly resisting Polish 10th Infantry Division. SS-Verfügungstruppe could be identified by a black-edged silver eagle of a design different from the Army's on their left shoulder, black collar tabs and shoulder straps, and a white decal shield bearing black SS runes on the helmet's right side. SS-Verfügungstruppe units committed to the fighting in Poland included the SS-Leibstandarte Adolf Hitler, SS-Standarte "Deutschland," SS-Standarte "Germania," and SS-Standarte "Der Führer."

Mountain troops (Gebirgstruppen), identifiable by the Edelweiss badge on their right sleeves, of the 14.Armee attacking into southern Poland from Slovakia pass though Rybnik-Mikolow within hours after crossing the frontier. Three mountain divisions were assigned to the 14.Armee, 1st, 2nd, and 3rd. Dead Polish troops litter the area.

A Pz.Kpfw.II Ausf.a1 of the 3.Panzer-Division rolls into action. The Pz.Kpfw.II Ausf.a1 was the first pre-production model of the Pz.Kpfw.II. Even though only 25 were built in 1936 and supplemented by improved models, it was still in use in September 1939. The Pz.Kpfw.II Ausf.a1 and other pre-production models (Ausf.a2, a3, b) had three pairs of small road wheels attached to a girder-type beam. The Germans committed 3,251 tanks to Poland (losses are in parentheses): Pz.Kpfw.I- 1,445 (89), Pz.Kpfw.II- 1,223 (78), Pz.Kpfw.III- 98 (26), Pz.Kpfw.IV- 211 (19), Pz.Kpfw.38(t)- 59 (6), plus 215 command tanks (losses unknown, possibly included with the basic models) of all types assigned to six Panzer and four light divisions plus a few odd separate units. The light divisions, essentially cavalry arm mechanized formations, would later be reorganized and redesignated Panzer divisions.

In an obviously posed photograph, 4.Armee troops fighting across the Polish Corridor are seen with two Volksdeutsch girls in the small town of Pruszcz just across the frontier. They display the black-white-red shield decal on the right side of the M35 helmets and the silver Wehrmacht eagle on a black shield on the left side. This appears to be a machine gun company owing to the number of pistol-armed soldiers, the machine gun spare parts case worn on one man's right front belt, and the heavy-duty hauling sling (with the large snap hook) on the left hip of the third man from the right. The shelter cape, usually worn attached to the back of the suspenders, is worn by some men in a roll over the left shoulder making them more accessible.

General der Panzertruppen Heinz Guderian commander of XIX.Armeekorps (2.Infanterie-Division [Motorized]), 3.Panzer-Division) observes developments at the front. Later to command a Panzer group (equivalent to a corps), then Inspector of Panzer Troops, finally became the Chief of the General Staff of the Army, he had pioneered the Blitzkrieg concept and the formation of the Panzer Arm. His tactics and concepts were to be proved in Poland, the Low Countries, France, and Russia.

The Germans employed a wide mix of armored reconnaissance cars, even at the beginning of the war. From left to right: a Sd.Kfz.222 (Sonderkraftfahrzeug—special motorized vehicle) cannon car with a 2cm automatic gun and an MG.34 machine gun, a Sd.Kfz.221 machine gun car with only one MG.34 machine gun, and a six-wheeled Sd.Kfz.231 armored car with the same armament as the Sd.Kfz.222. The white Balkenkreuz can faintly be seen on the vehicle fronts.

German soldiers, probably of a reconnaissance battalion, man captured diminutive Polish TKS tankettes. The camouflage is a olive drab and dark brown splinter pattern. The two-man TKS was nothing more than a machine carrier suitable only for reconnaissance and security patrols or providing infantry with covering fire. They were slow, inadequate on rough or muddy terrain, and very lightly protected with 3-10mm of armor. A 7.92mm Hotchkiss wz.25 machine gun was mounted in a non-rotating cupola. Poland possessed 574 TKSs and similar, but older TKs. Poland possessed only some 270 heavier tanks armed with 37mm or 47mm guns plus another 40 twin 7.92mm machine gun-armed light tanks, 100 entirely obsolete World War I French Renault FT-17 light tanks, and 100 7.92mm machine gun-armed, light armored scout cars. While the heavier Polish tanks were better armed than most German tanks, there were insufficient in number and too widely scattered among units to be effective.

A Sd.Kfz.265 small armor command vehicle, a light command tank built on the chassis of a Pz.Kpfw.I Ausf.A. The turret was removed and crew compartment built up to form a non-rotating superstructure with room for an additional man, the unit commander, a map table and larger radio, for which a low frame-type radio antenna was provided on this example. Its only armament was a ball-mounted MG.34 in the superstructure's right front.

A group (squad) of troops of SS-Standarte "Deutschland" pose sitting on the lip of a crater caused by a large-caliber Polish gun, possibly 12cm, fired from the Mlawa Position facing East Prussia, which had previously been unknown to the Germans. Defended by the Polish 20th Infantry Division, the fortress held out for three days. Anti-gas protection cape pouches are fastened to their gas mask carrier straps over their chests.

General Heinz Guderian, commanding the 4.Panzer-Division, passes a column of light tanks. In the foreground is a Pz.Kpfw.I Ausf.B followed by two Pz.Kpfw.II Ausf.As. Guderian utilized the Sd.Kfz.251/6 command vehicle (Befehlswagen) version of the medium rifleman's armor vehicle (mittlerer Schützenpanzerwagen—mSPW) complete with long-range radios and an Enigma cryptographic device.

This Polish 9.4-ton 7TPjw light tank was one of the best tanks possessed by the Poles. It was knocked out by a 3.7cm round dead through the center side portion of the hull. Owing to the fire damage it appears the ammunition detonated. Many Polish tanks were painted an olive drab base with dark brown and sand wavy band or blocked patterns. The 7TP design was influenced by the British Vickers E light tank, which Poland had purchased in 1931. The 7TPjw had a Bofors 3.7cm wz.37 gun and a Browning air-cooled 7.92mm wz.33 while the twin-turreted 7TPdw was armed with two Browning water-cooled 7.92mm wz.30 machine guns. Poland possessed 95 7TPjw and 40 7TPdw light tanks. These tanks equipped the 1st and 2nd Light Tank Battalions assigned to the High Command along with the 3rd Battalion equipped with French 3.7cm gun-armed R-35S tanks. As the French failed to do the following year, the Poles did not mass their armor units, but deployed them piecemeal.

German 3.Armee troops are enthusiastically greeted by the Volksdeutsche inhabitants of Dirschau in northern Poland. The artillerymen ride in a 5-ton capacity Sd.Kfz.6 halftrack used as a prime mover for 10.5cm howitzers and other light artillery in motorized and Panzer divisions. Note the helmet camouflage bands cut from automobile tire inner tubes.

3.Armee lieutenants and captains report to their battalion commander near Lowice as an artillery unit passes by. All wear pistols while the battalion commander additionally has a bayonet, referred to as a sidearm in the German Army. In most usage the term "sidearm" refers to handguns, which were called Handwaffen (hand weapons). Most of the officers wear the new-type field service cap. Officer leather equipment was mostly reddish brown while enlisted men's were black. Some officer's dyed their leather gear black though as the light reddish brown was too conspicuous.

Two infantrymen survey extensive damage, probably caused by air attack, to enemy positions near the Polish/German border on the first day of the campaign. Hundreds of unexploded Polish 15cm artillery shells litter the area, which must have been an ammunition dump.

This 2cm FlaK.30 light antiaircraft gun has been set up on top of what appears to be an old Polish border fortification giving a good overall vantage point against enemy aircraft. Both the dog and the gunner are taking it easy in the hot September sun. In the distance Polish prisoners can be seen filing across a bridge back into Germany.

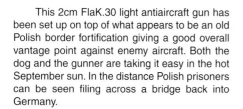

Massive traffic jams were a frequent occurrence during the invasion on the limited Polish road system. Here Polish prisoners of war are transported west by 8.Armee troops in Opel Blitz Type 2.5-32 trucks. This 1.5-ton capacity light truck was an adapted commercial design widely used by the German Army. Only the rear wheels were powered and this would prove inadequate in future campaigns.

Officers and staff NCOs observe the advance of their unit using binoculars and an artillery-type observation telescope. A cluster of hay stacks such as this made it easy for personnel to seek concealment if enemy aircraft appeared. An NCO serving as air guard in the rear peers skyward.

A Junkers Ju-52/3mg three-engine transport, commonly called the Tante Ju (Aunt Ju) or Alt eiser Tante (Old Iron Aunt) offloads a bicycle rifle unit on a recently captured airfield in western Poland. The standard troop bicycle (Truppenfahrrad) could be loaded with the personal equipment normally carried on the individual soldier. Items include a satchel-like clothing bag, canteen, mess kit, and stick hand grenades. The troop bicycle possessed such amenities as an equipment rack over the rear fender, a hand-operated air pump, a wheel-powered generator for the headlight, and a warning bell ringer. Bicycle troops could easily cover three or more times the distance of force-marching foot troops and arrive less tired.

Two Luftwaffe soldiers, probably flak troops according to the apparent red shade of their collar patches provide security at an airfield. They wear blue-gray uniforms and helmets. Beside their fighting position, known as a Wolfgrabhügel (wolf's barrow) to German soldiers, analogous to foxhole, is a three-color splinter camouflage shelter cape. The cape was reversible with darker shades of green and brown on one side and lighter shades on the other. A flight of Heinkel He-111 bombers takeoff to hit targets well inside Poland. Deeper targets were struck from 2 September to avoid accidentally attacking scattered advancing German units.

A column of Pz.Kpfw.I Ausf.B tanks pass infantrymen eating soup or stew (common field fair) beside a horse-drawn, wagon-mounted field kitchen. Food could be cooked in such field kitchens, known as a Gulaschkanone (goulash cannon) to the troops, as they were moved. The muddy road and troops wearing shelter capes indicate rainy weather. Note that the otherwise predominate white Balkenkreuzen on the tanks have been partly obscured by smeared mud. On the side of the nearest tank's turret are the numbers "523" identifying it as No. 3 tank in the 2nd Platoon of the 5th Company. The number did not identify the parent battalion. While this system was little used at the beginning of the war, it became universal the following year.

While much of an infantry division's support and service units were at least partly motorized and haul by horse-drawn wagons, a division's 27 rifle companies walked as they advanced deeper into Poland. The bicyclists are probably from the regiment's mounted platoon. Some of these platoons were provided horses, but many were equipped with bicycles requiring less care. The regimental mounted platoon was used for scouting, maintaining contact between dispersed elements, and as couriers.

A 4.Armee motorcycle rifle unit moves toward Bydgoszcz along a road, which saw a great deal of fighting during its clearing. Motorcycle rifle battalions were employed for reconnaissance and as exploitation units. Their high-speed mobility and good cross-country capabilities allowed them to take advantage of many situations in which it was necessary to gain a quick advantage such as seizing an abandoned bridge, securing a vital crossroads in advance of the main body, or screening an exposed flank as the main body raced ahead toward its objective ignoring by-passed enemy.

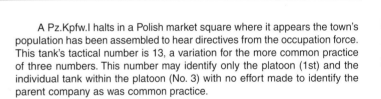

A Pz.Kpfw.I halts in a Polish market square where it appears the town's population has been assembled to hear directives from the occupation force. This tank's tactical number is 13, a variation for the more common practice of three numbers. This number may identify only the platoon (1st) and the individual tank within the platoon (No. 3) with no effort made to identify the parent company as was common practice.

A column of Czechoslovak-made Pz.Kpfw.38(t) light tanks (TNHP-S in Czechoslovak service) advance through a Polish village during the second day of hostilities. These tanks belong to the 3.leicht-Division, which had an extra battalion of 59 of these excellent tanks. Armed with a 3.7cm gun and two 7.92mm machine guns, as well as possessing much thicker armor, they were markedly superior to that of the Pz.Kpfw.I and II with their machine guns and 2cm cannons.

A motorized rifle group (squad) is mounted aboard a captured Polish light truck as they advance across the Tuchola Hearth. The diamond-shaped national insignia on the left front fender is red on white. At this time infantry regiments assigned to Panzer and light divisions were designated Schützen (Rifle), were not redesignated Panzergrenadier until 1942 while those designated Infanterie (motorisiert) were assigned to Infantry Divisions (Motorized) and were not redesignated as Panzergrenadier until 1944 even though their parent divisions had been redesignated Panzergrenadier in 1942.

The pilot and gunner climb aboard Messerschmitt Bf-110C long-range twin-engine fighter as they scramble to attack an enemy force. The Bf-110 was employed in the ground attack, anti-bomber, and bomber escort roles. It was initially an effective aircraft in all roles, until it encountered more maneuverable British single-engine fighters in 1940. Armament included two 20mm MG.FF cannons and four 7.92mm MG.17 machine guns in the nose and a 7.92mm MG.15 in the rear cockpit plus two 100kg (220-lb) bombs beneath each wing. The pilot wears a seat-type parachute while the gunner has a back-type providing him with more freedom of movement.

A 3.7cm PaK.35/36 antitank gun crew covers their regimental headquarters area established beside a lumber cutting camp. Regimental antitank companies were assigned 12 of these guns. PaK means Panzer-Abwehr-Kanone, or armor defense gun. In April 1940 Panzerabwehr units were redesignated Panzerjäger (armor hunter) in order to provide a less defensive sounding title in an army very much oriented to the offense. As better protected tanks were encountered in Russia the German soldier began calling the 3.7cm PaK the Torklopfer ("Doorknocker") in recognition of its limited armor penetration. The camouflage on this gun sitting in the open is only of limited effectiveness.

A motorcycle rifle (Kradschützen) unit dismounts from its solo and combination sidecar (Beiwagen) motorcycles (Kraftrad—abbreviated Krad) as it is engaged by Polish troops. When engaged the one or two riflemen aboard each motorcycle would dismount to maneuver against the enemy while the drivers withdrew to the first available cover to the rear and would then provide covering fire. The Germans employed a wide variety of motorcycles to include BMW, DKW, NSU, Triumph, Victoria, and Zündapp models.

An Sd.Kfz.8 halftrack of the 3.Panzer-Division crosses the Vistula River on a medium pontoon bridge (Brückengerät T). This 12-ton capacity vehicle was used as a prime mover for 15cm howitzers, 8.8cm and 10.5cm antiaircraft guns, and bridge section trailers.

Officers of the 11.Infanterie-Division and Panzerverband Kempf interrogate Polish prisoners near the Mlawa Position. Note the NCO opening a map in order to locate the whereabouts of the withdrawing enemy forces in the area. Polish uniforms were a light olive drab with the brown predominating.

Two SS-Verfügungstruppe NCOs of Panzerverband Kempf speak with a dispatch rider wearing the motorcycle rider's protective coat, a gray-green rubberized canvas ankle-length coat. They stand beside a makeshift bridge crossing a stream on the road to Chorzele. The Totenkopf (death head) badge and the SS eagle adorn their old-style field service caps with black bands.

A German cannonieer removes the shipping plug from a 15cm high explosive projectile to install the fuse. The battalion prepares to go into action against Polish positions east of Bydgoszcz. A battalion of 15cm sFH 18 medium field howitzers armed each division's medium artillery battalion to back the three 10.5cm field howitzer battalions. In motorized divisions the 15cm was towed by halftrack prime movers. In infantry divisions they were horse-drawn in two loads, the two-wheel carriage and trails supported by a two-wheel limber and the tube of a special four-wheel wagon.

German soldiers of the 3.Armee are greeted by Volksdeutsch women who offer smiles and food to their liberators. This unit has fabricated helmet camouflage covers from burlap cloth and their camouflage shelter capes are worn as blanket rolls over their left shoulders.

A motorcycle sidecar combination followed by a Horch staff car passes soldiers repairing a dirt by-pass road leading from a temporary pioneer bridge quickly laid beside a totally destroyed highway bridge.

Soldiers of the 50.Infanterie-Division cross the canal at the edge of Bydgoszcz. It was a common practice for pioneer troops to hastily construct temporary footbridges laid across the wreckage of downed bridges to keep the infantry moving forward. Unusually, these troops are marching across a difficult route with their bayonets fixed.

The first few days of combat had brought about an exhilarating aura of adventure. The great majority of soldiers had never seen action, and approached the campaign with an eagerness that promised much to their commanders. But it sometimes came with a price–their life. Here in western Poland near Poznan a wooden cross and a M35 helmet marks the spot where a young German soldier is buried after giving all to the Fatherland.

3.Armee troops cross the Narew River as they continue the advance. Here Hf.1 light field wagons cross a pontoon bridge following in the wake on the infantry. German infantry divisions relied on several company-size supply transport columns carrying ammunition, fuel, rations, and other supplies. An infantry division typically had almost 5,400 horses for this purpose and for towing artillery. The Hf.1 light field wagon was 3.86 meters long, the Hf.2 heavy field wagon was 4.24 meters long, and the Hf.3 small field wagon was 3.25 meters long.

Spare draft horses are herded by bicyclists across the same Narew River pontoon bridge. Divisional motorized elements are now crossing, possibly a signal unit. Note the vehicles on the far shore are somewhat dispersed. This was a dangerous point in time with vehicle columns jammed up at the crossing site's chokepoint. Such a concentration in a small area was a lucrative target for aircraft and artillery, although by this time there was little threat from the former.

An infantryman grabs sleep when and where he can. The relentless push across Poland allowed little time for rest. This worn-out rifle platoon provides an excellent display of individual and unit equipment including dispatch cases, binocular case, steel gas mask carriers, canteens, mess kits, small entrenching tools, and bread bags. A machine gun ammunition bearer sits in the road atop a pair of ammunition boxes each holding six 50-round belts or a 250-round belt. The prone machine gunner uses his helmet and MG.34 as a read rest.

The crews of a 2cm cannon-armed Sd.Kfz.222 (left) and a 7.92mm machine gun-armed Sd.Kfz.221 (right) armored car service and refuel their vehicles. It was common for the vehicles to be mixed in the same unit. Constantly on the move it was vital that in order not to jeopardize their rapid thrust eastward they tried not to overstretch their lines of communication and outrun their following supply columns. Like tank crewmen, armored car crews worn the black Panzer uniform and black beret, beneath which was a padded protective liner. The arm of service piping color for Panzer troops was pink.

A heavy machine gun group (squad) relaxes by playing cards, most likely the highly popular skat, beside their MG.34 set up on the high antiaircraft adapter for the standard tripod mount 34. In German service the terms light and heavy machine guns defined role and not the weight of the gun, as both roles were filled by the MG.34. Rifle groups had a light machine gun with a bipod and carried one or two spare barrels. A heavy machine gun group also had the bipod-fitted machine gun, but additionally carried a heavy tripod, an optical sight, and additional spare barrels to provide long-range, sustained fire.

In contrast to understandably enthusiastic Volksdeutschen, glum looking Poles watch a XXI.Armeekorps wagon supply transport column pass through their village near Grudziadz. Once Grudziadz was secured the pioneer troops immediately began replacing the Vistula River bridges to link up with 4.Armee.

Unterfeldwebel, 1.Gebirgsjäger-Division, Lemberg, South Poland

The mountain troops distinguished themselves as an elite infantry formation in Poland. The fundamental difference between standard German infantryman and mountain troops, was the wearing of the cloth Edelweiss sleeve insignia on the right arm of his field blouse, the stone-grey mountain trousers modeled on the civilian ski trouser (Keilhose) design, the heavily studded & cleated mountain boots with wool putties, and the regulation (Bergmutze) mountain field cap with its unique Edelweiss metal badge on the left side. In this case the M35 steel helmet is being worn due to combat conditions. The steel helmet is adorned by two decals on either side showing the national colors decal (in early 1940 this highly conspicuous decal was to be removed, the M35 helmets smooth semi-gloss field-grey look was to be changed to a more combat welcoming rough-texture darker matt grey).

The smart looking M35 & M36 field blouse was standard issue to all German army personnel in 1939 with the national emblem on a dark green base sewn on the right breast. There were no major differences between these two types of tunics, apart from an inside alteration to the lining of the M36 field blouse for better wear. Typical of these tunics was the dark-green facing collar made from badge cloth. The decorative army collar Litzen insignia incorporates two light-green central stripes (branch color indicating Gebirgsjäger). This color in piping (waffenfarbe) was worn around the shoulder straps. The field blouse was made from a field–grey quality cloth with a high woollen content. However it would be more accurate to describe the color of the pre-war field blouse as field-green. Due to security reasons, and unique to this campaign, he has buttoned the grey cloth attachment tap over the dark-green shoulder strap to camouflage his regimental number (in 1940 shoulder straps were manufactured without regimental numbers). Characteristic of senior NCOs he wears bright aluminum tresse trim on his collar and on his shoulder straps.

This Squad Leader (Sergeant) carries the equipment & weapons bestowed to his rank. He is issued with the Karabiner 98k; the standard rifle used by NCOs and enlisted men. In 1939 machine-pistols were in short supply and only issued to specialist troops therefore infantry squad leaders had to make do with the rifle. Being a senior NCO he was issued with a P08 pistol and 6x30 field binoculars with carrying case. Attached to his army leather belt are the NCO's M1935 dispatch case (one of several variants) and a Kar 98k ammunition pouch. Out of view he would have also been issued basic infantry equipment, the M1931 breadbag, M1931 field flask with drinking cup and M31 (Zeltbahn) shelter quarter, small entrenching tool, S84/98 bayonet with leather frog and gasmask in its M1930 metal canister.

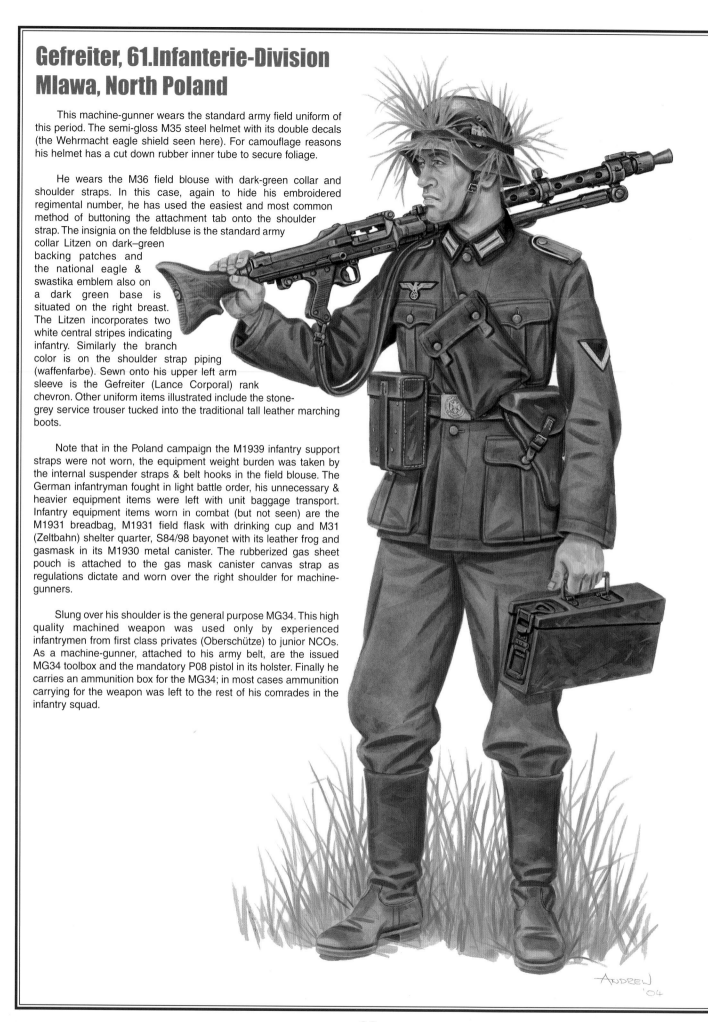

Gefreiter, 61.Infanterie-Division Mlawa, North Poland

This machine-gunner wears the standard army field uniform of this period. The semi-gloss M35 steel helmet with its double decals (the Wehrmacht eagle shield seen here). For camouflage reasons his helmet has a cut down rubber inner tube to secure foliage.

He wears the M36 field blouse with dark-green collar and shoulder straps. In this case, again to hide his embroidered regimental number, he has used the easiest and most common method of buttoning the attachment tab onto the shoulder strap. The insignia on the feldbluse is the standard army collar Litzen on dark–green backing patches and the national eagle & swastika emblem also on a dark green base is situated on the right breast. The Litzen incorporates two white central stripes indicating infantry. Similarly the branch color is on the shoulder strap piping (waffenfarbe). Sewn onto his upper left arm sleeve is the Gefreiter (Lance Corporal) rank chevron. Other uniform items illustrated include the stone-grey service trouser tucked into the traditional tall leather marching boots.

Note that in the Poland campaign the M1939 infantry support straps were not worn, the equipment weight burden was taken by the internal suspender straps & belt hooks in the field blouse. The German infantryman fought in light battle order, his unnecessary & heavier equipment items were left with unit baggage transport. Infantry equipment items worn in combat (but not seen) are the M1931 breadbag, M1931 field flask with drinking cup and M31 (Zeltbahn) shelter quarter, S84/98 bayonet with its leather frog and gasmask in its M1930 metal canister. The rubberized gas sheet pouch is attached to the gas mask canister canvas strap as regulations dictate and worn over the right shoulder for machine-gunners.

Slung over his shoulder is the general purpose MG34. This high quality machined weapon was used only by experienced infantrymen from first class privates (Oberschütze) to junior NCOs. As a machine-gunner, attached to his army belt, are the issued MG34 toolbox and the mandatory P08 pistol in its holster. Finally he carries an ammunition box for the MG34; in most cases ammunition carrying for the weapon was left to the rest of his comrades in the infantry squad.

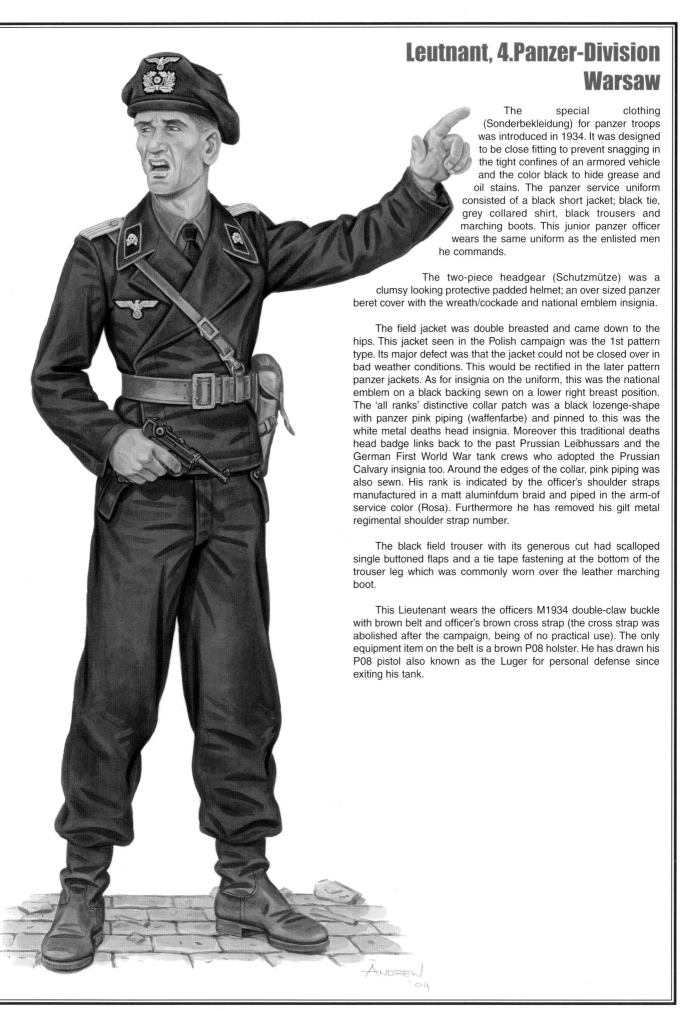

Leutnant, 4.Panzer-Division Warsaw

The special clothing (Sonderbekleidung) for panzer troops was introduced in 1934. It was designed to be close fitting to prevent snagging in the tight confines of an armored vehicle and the color black to hide grease and oil stains. The panzer service uniform consisted of a black short jacket; black tie, grey collared shirt, black trousers and marching boots. This junior panzer officer wears the same uniform as the enlisted men he commands.

The two-piece headgear (Schutzmütze) was a clumsy looking protective padded helmet; an over sized panzer beret cover with the wreath/cockade and national emblem insignia.

The field jacket was double breasted and came down to the hips. This jacket seen in the Polish campaign was the 1st pattern type. Its major defect was that the jacket could not be closed over in bad weather conditions. This would be rectified in the later pattern panzer jackets. As for insignia on the uniform, this was the national emblem on a black backing sewn on a lower right breast position. The 'all ranks' distinctive collar patch was a black lozenge-shape with panzer pink piping (waffenfarbe) and pinned to this was the white metal deaths head insignia. Moreover this traditional deaths head badge links back to the past Prussian Leibhussars and the German First World War tank crews who adopted the Prussian Calvary insignia too. Around the edges of the collar, pink piping was also sewn. His rank is indicated by the officer's shoulder straps manufactured in a matt aluminfdum braid and piped in the arm-of service color (Rosa). Furthermore he has removed his gilt metal regimental shoulder strap number.

The black field trouser with its generous cut had scalloped single buttoned flaps and a tie tape fastening at the bottom of the trouser leg which was commonly worn over the leather marching boot.

This Lieutenant wears the officers M1934 double-claw buckle with brown belt and officer's brown cross strap (the cross strap was abolished after the campaign, being of no practical use). The only equipment item on the belt is a brown P08 holster. He has drawn his P08 pistol also known as the Luger for personal defense since exiting his tank.

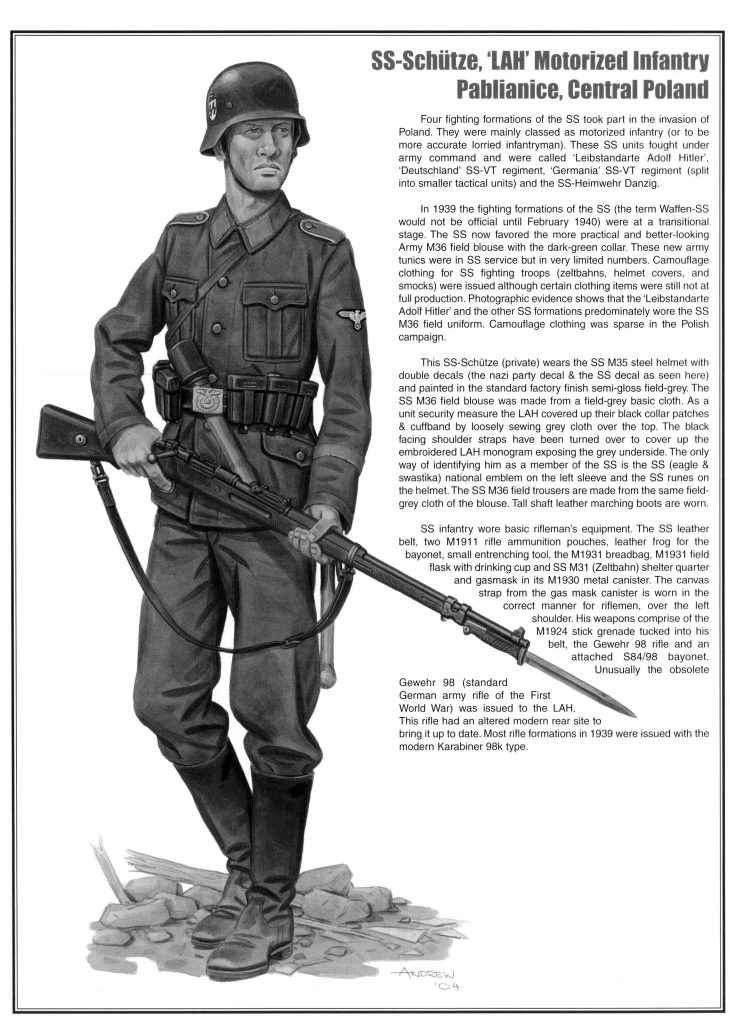

SS-Schütze, 'LAH' Motorized Infantry Pablianice, Central Poland

Four fighting formations of the SS took part in the invasion of Poland. They were mainly classed as motorized infantry (or to be more accurate lorried infantryman). These SS units fought under army command and were called 'Leibstandarte Adolf Hitler', 'Deutschland' SS-VT regiment, 'Germania' SS-VT regiment (split into smaller tactical units) and the SS-Heimwehr Danzig.

In 1939 the fighting formations of the SS (the term Waffen-SS would not be official until February 1940) were at a transitional stage. The SS now favored the more practical and better-looking Army M36 field blouse with the dark-green collar. These new army tunics were in SS service but in very limited numbers. Camouflage clothing for SS fighting troops (zeltbahns, helmet covers, and smocks) were issued although certain clothing items were still not at full production. Photographic evidence shows that the 'Leibstandarte Adolf Hitler' and the other SS formations predominately wore the SS M36 field uniform. Camouflage clothing was sparse in the Polish campaign.

This SS-Schütze (private) wears the SS M35 steel helmet with double decals (the nazi party decal & the SS decal as seen here) and painted in the standard factory finish semi-gloss field-grey. The SS M36 field blouse was made from a field-grey basic cloth. As a unit security measure the LAH covered up their black collar patches & cuffband by loosely sewing grey cloth over the top. The black facing shoulder straps have been turned over to cover up the embroidered LAH monogram exposing the grey underside. The only way of identifying him as a member of the SS is the SS (eagle & swastika) national emblem on the left sleeve and the SS runes on the helmet. The SS M36 field trousers are made from the same field-grey cloth of the blouse. Tall shaft leather marching boots are worn.

SS infantry wore basic rifleman's equipment. The SS leather belt, two M1911 rifle ammunition pouches, leather frog for the bayonet, small entrenching tool, the M1931 breadbag, M1931 field flask with drinking cup and SS M31 (Zeltbahn) shelter quarter and gasmask in its M1930 metal canister. The canvas strap from the gas mask canister is worn in the correct manner for riflemen, over the left shoulder. His weapons comprise of the M1924 stick grenade tucked into his belt, the Gewehr 98 rifle and an attached S84/98 bayonet. Unusually the obsolete Gewehr 98 (standard German army rifle of the First World War) was issued to the LAH. This rifle had an altered modern rear site to bring it up to date. Most rifle formations in 1939 were issued with the modern Karabiner 98k type.

ANDREW '04

Pioneer troops stand beside their recently completed prefabricated bridge as a Sd.Kfz.265 small armor command vehicle (Befehlspanzer) crosses. The six 4-meter assault bridge equipment (Brückengerät) sections, carried by pioneer units aboard truck and halftracks, provide the off-ramp on to a corduroy road (log matting laid across a dirt road to prevent it from being churned into mud). Many tanks were painted dark gray overall, but a dark brown "cloud" camouflage pattern was also used of about one-third brown coverage. In black and white photographs it is often difficult to discern these two-color camouflage patterns.

This Ju-52/3mg transport was more likely to have been brought down by antiaircraft fire by this stage of the campaign. The Germans often recovered such aircraft to rebuild or salvage for parts and recycle the valuable aluminum and steel components.

A unit commander in a Horch staff car, possibly a regimental commander, peers down a side street searching for enemy activity. German commanders frequently conducted personal reconnaissance, often at great risk. Motorcyclists were assigned to unit headquarters to serve as escorts and dispatch riders. The damage here appears to have been caused by the Luftwaffe.

The commander of a Pz.Kpfw.I Ausf.A (four road wheels, other types had five and a lengthened hull) observes his route for enemy activity before advancing further. Foliage attached to a tank provides little camouflage if moving, but if halted it offers some degree of concealment from distant ground and air observers. MG.34 machine guns installed in Pz.Kpfw.Is habitually lacked flash suppressors.

A 3.7cm PaK.35/36 anti-tank gun crew providing covering fire as an unidentified old-type armored car approaches. The log cabin farmhouse may have been set aflame by artillery or tracer fire. Contrary to popular belief, the Luftwaffe in Poland did not provide the constant bombardment that was needed. Much was credited to the use of artillery, despite it being seriously criticized after the campaign.

Casualties are loaded aboard a Ju-52/3mg transport at a northern Poland airfield and bound for Breslau. Although casualties were not excessive in most units, a number of commanders became increasingly concerned at the growing numbers of wounded. Partisan warfare was also increasing and beginning to take a small toll. The dorsal position for the transport's sole protective armament, a 7.92mm MG.15 machine gun, can be seen.

A Pz.Kpfw.IV Ausf.A halts outside a town in western Poland. The few Pz.Kpfw.IVs in use were envisioned as infantry support tanks explaining their low-velocity, short-barreled 7.5cm gun referred to as a Stumpf (Stumpy). It was better suited for knocking out pillboxes, strongpoints, and fortified buildings than enemy tanks. The Pz.Kpfw.IV though would become the most widely used German tank and later models would be provided with long-barrel 7.5cm guns. The piece of equipment attached to the track guard below the forward seated crewman is a jack for reinstalling thrown or replacing damaged tracks.

A Pz.Kpfw.I Ausf.A clatters through a Polish street. The white Balkenkreuzen have been painted over to deny the enemy an aim point. One Polish weapon that came as a surprise was the 7.92mm wz.35 antitank rifle. These were secretly held in unit armories until the invasion. While small in caliber, the armor-piercing bullet was backed by a massive cartridge case and could penetrate over 30mm of armor at 100 meters and easily punched through the light armor of the Pz.Kpfw.I and II.

Pushing southward toward the Narew River, these I.Armeekorps infantrymen march through yet another demolished town. The company train with immediate use reserve ammunition and rations follows them. By the appearance of their uniforms these may be freshly committed reserves. Note that each soldier is wearing a gas protective cape in the flat pouch attached to the gas mask carrier shoulder strap.

German infantrymen watch as a Polish town is consumed by fire. Most of the remaining pockets of resistance have already been neutralized by the pulverizing affects of air attack. Through the dust and smoke endless streams of bombers could still be seen droning slowly towards the target areas.

German troops eat a rushed meal beside a captured Polish TKS tanklette on which a white Balkenkreuz was crudely painted. For these soldiers food was the readiest form of sustaining morale among the troops in Poland. The thought of a home cooked meal came to seem an unimaginable luxury. Although many men came to detest the rations, it was the monotony of the food that the soldiers cursed, rather than its quality. Note that some of the soldiers wear civilian shirts under their tunics.

A wounded motorcyclist is brought in to a medical post for treatment in a BMW's sidecar. The 10x20cm (the standard size) white unit symbol on the front of the sidecar indicates it belongs to a motorized infantry staff company. This is the same tactical symbol as used on maps and was a common practice. In the background is a Krupp L2H43 light truck, the most commonly used by motorized infantry units.

A week of continuous combat and non-stop movement was beginning to take its toll on men, horses, and equipment. Panzerverband Kempf's rapid advance north of Warsaw was extremely exhausting as the troops were compelled to be on the move day and night. A dispatch rider is sleeping on the roadside next to his motorcycle still wearing his helmet and waterproof motorcycle protective coat. His personal equipment is striped to the motorcycle's rear rack.

Equally exhausted, a horse and rider rest during 8.Armee's advance to Lodz. Forward of the M25 saddle are M34 saddlebags. The rider carries his one canteen and another for the horse is attached to the saddle. This is not a cavalry unit as cavalry branch color was gold yellow and the piping chevron on the front of the field cap is a dark color, possibly indicating an artillery (red) or pioneer (black) unit.

German infantry, completely exhausted after seven days of almost continuous fighting and marching, take a break by the roadside. Note the hobnails on the marching riding boots. The rightmost soldier is wearing spurs and is probably the lead horse rider for the light equipment cart above them.

This may be a staged propaganda photograph showing infantrymen and a Pz.Kpfw.II conducting a night attack, which seldom occurred. A great number of photographs during what came to be known in propaganda films, such as the Eighteen Day Victory March,* were purely aimed at showing the German population the victorious German advance through Poland.

* The Nazi 18-day claim was pure propaganda. The last Polish troops surrendered on 6 October.

The crew of a 15cm sFH 18 heavy field howitzer wait during a pause in fighting. Some battalions armed with this weapon had three four-gun batteries. The 15cm had a range of 13,325 meters. The wooden frames to the right contain projectiles and those to the right are propellant canisters.

Two Pz.Kpfw.I tanks of the 4.Panzer-Division reaches the suburbs of Warsaw. Panzer-Regiment.35 was the first unit to arrive on the outskirts of the capital. The white crosses on the tanks have been partially obscured to make them less conspicuous targets. On the hull side below the driver's hatch is a detachable plate with the individual tank identification number, but a more visible tactical numbers has been painted in larger numbers on the turret side. The pre-war plates allowed the plates to be attached to available vehicles for training.

A Sd.Kfz.10 light halftrack (leichter Zugkraftwagen) of XV.Motorized-Korps passes over a prefabricated wooden bridge west of Warsaw and would enter Warsaw the nest day. After advancing over 140 miles in one week, these units were exhausted but determined to capture Warsaw. This light halftrack was used to tow 3.7cm antitank guns and 2cm antiaircraft guns.

Advanced elements of Division Reinhardt move into the suburbs of Warsaw using a Pz.Kpfw.II Ausf.A as cover. The "R05" tactical number identifies the tank as belonging to a regimental staff officer. The regimental commander's tank would be identified by "R05." For the attack into the suburbs of the city two assault groups were formed. Gefechtsgruppe I (combat group) was built around Panzer-Regiment.35 to capture the Ochota suburb. At the same time Gefechtsgruppe II, formed around Panzer-Regiment.36, directed its forces against the Wola district.

A group of Pz.Kpfw.I Ausf.A halt in a street under heavy Polish fire during Division Reinhardt's push into Warsaw. These tanks were part of Panzer-Regiment.35 during the battle for the Ochota suburb. Note that by this time the tank's tactical number was more predominately displayed on the turret in order to make control easier. Despite the losses sustained during the first assaults on the city white crosses are still evident on many tanks. Polish antitank rifles and guns inflicted heavy losses in the rubble of Warsaw.

After the heavy bombardment by SS artillery on the town of Rozan, SS-Standarte "Deutschland" and Panzer-Regiment.7 conducted a series of assaults on the town against strongly defended enemy positions. Almost every building in the path of the attack was destroyed by mortars and artillery, until the enemy had been worn down by attrition.

German soldiers inspect the complete destruction of Rozan on 8 September. Hundreds of towns and villages were subjected to similar bombings and shelling. The Poles that fled from Rozan knew their forces were being inexorably ground down and that they could not hope for reinforcements. Already some Polish battalions had been broken up to fill the dwindling ranks of others in the line.

More vehicles from SS-Standarte "Deutschland" and Panzer-Regiment.7 file through the destroyed town of Rozan. After the heavy unrelenting fighting for Rozan the SS advance flowed again in the direction of Loriza through a succession of hot, dust-filled days and rainy nights until they reached Czervin and Hadbory. An Opel Blitz truck is parked here.

Officers of the divisional staff moving up the line towards Rozan in what appears to be a Mercedes-Benz staff car. The Wehrmacht as a whole used a wide variety of staff, or what were designated, light cars, including BMW, Hanomag, Mercedes-Benz, Skoda, Steyr, Stoewer, and Tatra makes as well as others commandeered from other occupied areas in many different models. Staff cars were usually dark grey or field grey (with the green predominating), but other retained their original civilian colors, though these would be overprinted when time allowed. The autumn weather, coupled with insistent rain, was cooling and necessitated the wear of field grey greatcoats.

In Govorovo vehicles and guns from Panzerverband Kempf roar past a 3.7cm antitank gun crew to cross the Naraw River. 10.5cm IFH 18 light field howitzers are drawn by Sd.Kfz. 6 halftracks.

Armed with a Mauser 7.92mm Kar.98k carbine, a German soldier from Panzerverband Kempf crosses a bridge over the Narew River in the town of Govorovo leaving behind a scene of total carnage and devastation in his wake. Poland used the very similar Polish license-produced Mauser wz.29 carbine. Germany and Poland both used the same 7.92mm cartridge in their carbines and machine guns.

German infantry accompanying Panzer-Regiment.36 take cover from heavy Polish resistance inside the suburb of Wola. Note the soldier with a short-handled folding entrenching tool. This was worn hanging from a belt, the blade of the shovel being held in a special open leather case. By now Warsaw laid bare, shrouded in dust and smoke from artillery shelling by both sides and incessant German bombing. Following continuous unceasing action German infantrymen, tankers, and gunners were totally exhausted after three days of battling in the suburbs. With the losses XVI.Armeekorps suffered during the Bzura counteroffensive, only a fraction of the 4.Panzer-Division, with the support of the SS-Leibstandarte "Adolf Hitler," was assigned to Warsaw.

German soldiers of 30.Infanterie-Division negotiate their way though a bomb-cratered town during the battle of the Bzura. All morning German troops reinforced by tanks repeatedly attacked Polish defenses. Now that the Polish Lodz Army had been forced away from Warsaw by XVI.Armeekorps, it had denied the Poles success in the Bzura area.

NCOs intently read an Army newspaper, Front Schau (Front Inspection) with the headline reporting that German forces have reached Warsaw, and were concluding their victorious march with its capture. Unknown to many, Reinhardt had already aborted an attack with Panzer-Regiments.35 and 36 the day before, and had lost 57 tanks in the process. Warsaw would continue to resist the might of the Wehrmacht until the 27 September. These NCOs wear the early style pointed-end shoulders straps without arm of service piping, which were being replaced by a rounded-end version with arm of service colored piping around the edges. The individual over the newspaper is an NCO aspirant (Unteroffizier Anwärter) identified by silver braid loop at the base of his shoulder strap.

Here German 10.Armee troops use a cart abandoned by fleeing inhabitants as cover to engage a Polish rearguard fighting from inside a shattered house on the other side of the square. This type of combat was typical during the German advance across Poland. Although in some areas the Poles managed to hold on regardless of the cost, the Polish army was still much shaken by the ferocity of the German assaults. Polish forces that were trapped inside the Radom pocket were cut off and besieged by infantry and tanks. By this date bridges across the Vistula River were successfully captured by IV.Armeekorps between Annopol and Deblin, including the important bridge at Pulawy. Schwedier Korps crossed the river, directing his troops toward Lublin, while XIV.Armeekorps was instructed to remain west of the Vistula and conduct a general mop-up of the remaining enemy troops still attempting to cross the Vistula.

An Sd.Kfz.265 small armor command vehicle of Panzer-Regiment.7 attached to Panzerverband Kempf drives off a dirt track towards the town of Siedlce. The black-on-white pennant displays the death head insignia of the SS. The triangular framework on the hull side is a rack for radio antenna sections.

Pz.Kpfw.Is and IIs of the Panzer-Regiment.7 advance further into north-central Poland. Paved road were scare in many areas. Such roads, under constant heavy wheeled and tracked vehicle traffic were ground into mud with the increasing autumn rains. The light car to the left bears the outlined rectangle with a side projection identifying it as a signal unit. Not that the dust has been whipped off the Balkenkreuz to make it more visible. The removal or obscuring of the crosses was inconsistent within even the same unit.

From 10 September and for the following few days the encircled Polish forces frantically attacked towards Lodz, but they could make no headway and changed the direction of their attack. These renewed assaults by the Poles were particularly heavy against the Kampfgruppe (battle group) consisting of SS-Leibstandarte "Adolph Hitler," II.Bataillon of Panzer-Regiment.33, and II.Bataillon of Panzer-Artillerie-Regiment.4. Over the next days that followed the Leibstandarte, supported by tanks, attacked towards the high ground west of Btonie, then stormed Kaputy, and fought a bitter confrontation at Sochaczew. Following in the wake of the Leibstandarte, soldiers from 30.Infanterie-Division pass through devastated Sochaczew, which changed hands more than four times, until it finally fell to the Germans. Infantrymen follow a Sd.Kfz.263 armored radio vehicle. By now infantrymen were fighting in the bear essential equipment with their unneeded gear being carried in the company train.

Three exhausted infantry NCOs sleep after the successful capture of Radom following continuous marching and fighting through Poland. These men probably of IV.Armeekorps, which had pinned the Polish troops in front of the city. The mechanized forces of XIV.Armeekorps then encircled the Poles from both north and south of Radom and captured almost 60,000 prisoners in the process.

A column of vehicles passes through the captured town of Radom. Strafing attacks probably killed the dead horses lying on the cobbled road.

12 September 1939

Later on 22 September at Wyskow Hitler reviewed the situation of 3.Armee under its commander, General of Artillery Georg von Küchler. During this short visit the Führer inspected a Polish armored train that had been destroyed by a Ju-87 attack. A Skoda 10cm wz.14/19P howitzer turret of this train can be seen above the heads of the entourage. Poland had possessed 10 armored trains and used them to good effect as mobile artillery. Some were destroyed by air attack and others were captured when encircled in a pocket and cut-off when the Luftwaffe knocked out railroad bridges.

Aboard Hitler's personal train code-named Führersonderzug F (Leader Special Train) in Poland on 12 September. Hitler with Chef des Wehrmachtführungsstab (Chief of the Defense Forces Command Staff), General of Artillery Alfred Jodl and Chef des Oberkommandos der Wehrmacht (High Command of the Defense Forces), General Field Marshall Wilhelm Keitel. They view the progress of the German armies in Poland on his visit to Army Group North headquarters. The following day Hitler visited the northern limits of the city of Lodz and made a trip to X.Armeekorps. On 15 September Hitler traveled further south and visited 14.Armee Headquarters and observed the crossing of the San River on a bridge built by German pioneers.

A 10cm sK.18 heavy gun pounds enemy positions somewhere in central Poland. Some divisional 15cm howitzer battalions also possessed a four-gun 10cm (actually 105mm) battery for counterbattery employment. It was mounted on the same carriage as the 15cm sFH 18, but had a much longer barrel. The 10cm had a range of 19,075 meters, almost 6,000 meters further than the companion 15cm howitzer.

This group of soldiers, based on their relaxed stance and complete lack of combat equipment and weapons, indicates they are in a secure situation watching their artillery pound Polish resistance. The hasty barricade served as an out guard position for the main defensive barricade stretching across the road further away.

Two artillery forward observers assess the effectiveness of fire of an artillery bombardment directed on burning factory. The observer to the left uses a 1-meter Em.R.1m rangefinder. Heavily constructed, multi-level factories were ideal for strongpoints. Resistance in a number of areas were still fierce and the defenders had to be destroyed, sometimes by completely razing the target area.

Although the outskirts of Warsaw had been secured, beleaguered Polish soldiers made a number of savage attacks on Mokotov, supported by tanks. Through the wreckage and debris of previous battles, the Poles charged into a barrage of German fire. Although there were many casualties among the Poles, the superior weight of the Polish infantry charges managed to overrun German strongpoints. SS soldiers, still engaged in house-to-house fighting since the previous day, were also driven from their positions. The Germans were forced to commit their few remaining reserves and the fighting continued for the rest of the day. Here German infantrymen force their way through the battered suburbs of Warsaw.

The battle of Warsaw had been a brutal contest between the attackers and the city's defenders. This is the Pz.Kpfw.III Ausf.B command tank of the commander of the Panzerverband Kempf (4.Panzer-Brigade). The Balkenkreuz appears to be dull yellow outlined in white. The yellow "B01" turret number identifies it as the brigade commander's tank.

German vehicles from 8.Armee halt inside a deserted village near the Bzura River. The Germans were now dominating almost every road leading out of the Bzura and Kutno region. Lines of infantry transport extended for miles and armor strengthened the various thrusts towards Kutno. Artillery batteries were positioned to shell Polish positions. The Poles were terribly shaken by the growing effectiveness of the German attacks and concentrated on escaping east to Warsaw. The faint rectangular box enclosing an "X" symbol on the rear of the light truck indicates it bellows to a divisional services unit.

13 September 1939

An SS officer, accompanied by a guard, explains the new order to Polish civilians. German occupation authorities were brutal and regulations were strictly enforced. Poland would soon loose its identity as a nation with almost a quarter of its territory absorbed into the Reich, over half taken over by the Soviet Union, and almost a quarter designated the Generalgouvernement (General Government) with the intend of it becoming a vast slave labor pool for Germany.

On the road to the Bzura River an officer of the 30.Infanterie-Division is apparently none too happy about having his photograph taken. Initially the Division made a rapid advance eastward, but was subsequently halted and ordered to assist to 10.Armee, which was meeting heavy resistance near Warsaw.

14 September 1939

Polish prisoners are interrogated by their captors. By now the Polish Army were militarily doomed. Dominated by increasing losses, Polish field commanders had become sodden with defeatism. Their units were in a pitiful shape with many breaking up, low on or having exhausted their ammunition and rations, their armor and artillery support destroyed, there was little they could do to further resist as some units fell back to eastern Poland or simply surrendered in increasing numbers.

German soldiers of XXII.Armeekorps edge forward under Polish fire west of the city of Lwów. A 7.92mm MG.13 machine gun crew fires on enemy positions around the base of a coal mine's waste heap. The Dreyse MG.13 used either 25-round box magazines or 75-round saddle drum magazines. It was the standard light machine gun during the Reichsheer-era, but many remained in use with mobilized reserve units as there were insufficient MG.34s available.

The reality of the German invasion of Poland. Polish partisans are lined up in the shadow of a farmhouse to be shot. German executions of soldiers and partisans alike were common as were the shooting of civilians as reprisals. Partisan warfare in Poland became one of the major threats to the German advance late in the campaign. They were detested and feared as much for the strain that they caused to men's routine movements in forward areas as for the casualties that they inflicted. The partisan practice of attacking lone stranded crews of tanks and other vehicles broken down on roads particularly enraged the Germans.

15 September 1939

By 2 September the Luftwaffe dominated the skies above Poland, but enemy air attacks by a few brave Polish fighter pilots were still able to cause disruption to a number of German units around Warsaw. Here the crew of a Luftwaffe 2cm FlaK.30 light antiaircraft gun secures an airfield. German Army light flak units also employed these automatic cannons.

A Sd.Kfz.6 halftrack towing a 10.5cm IFH 18, the standard drives toward the front on the Bzura River. Following is a Horch staff car. Each vehicle assign to the Wehrmacht was identified by a registration number bourn on a black-on-white plate on both the vehicle's front and rear. Those assigned to the Army were identified by "WH"- Wehrmacht Heer, those to the Luftwaffe by "WL"- Wehrmacht Luftwaffe, to the War Navy by WM"- Wehrmacht Kriegsmarine, and to the SS by runic lightening bolts (the SS was not a component of the Wehrmacht).

German officers in a small town on the Bzura River observe the aftermath of their one-hour artillery bombardment. With the continual build-up of German forces around the Bzura region, Polish forces under the command of General Kutrzeba were beginning to disintegrate. Now that the Lodz Army had been forced away from Warsaw by XVI.Armeekorps, it had finally denied the Poles success in the Bzura region. It was now only a matter of time before they were totally destroyed.

16 September 1939

A commander and staff of a supply column of Panzerveband Kempf discuss upcoming moves in yet another deserted village just north of Warsaw. Both SS-Verfügungstruppe and Army officers are seen in this photograph.

Officers of XVIII.Armeekorps receive orders for new front line mission around the city of Lwów. The Korps had moved up to Lwów and swung around the city, followed by XXII.Armeekorps, which immediately counter-attacked three Polish divisions to the east, west, and south of Lwów. Heavy artillery was brought to bear on enemy strongpoints around the heavily defended city, but the Poles were vastly superior in numbers and German forces found it difficult to extract them. The unit adjutant to the extreme left is identified by his dull silver cord aiguillette.

18 September 1939

Troops from Panzerverband Kempf watch Warsaw burn following a series of heavy bombardments by the Luftwaffe. Around Warsaw infantry divisions from three armies were able to impose a decisive blockade on the city's perimeter and prevent the bulk of the enemy escaping into the capital. Throughout the day heavy skirmishing continued with forays mounted by German units which probing pockets of resistance inside Warsaw's ravaged suburbs.

A Daimler-Benz G5 light truck leads a column through a blasted town east of the San River. This vehicle displays a white triangular tactical symbol on right fender indicates the vehicle belongs to the 4.Kompanie of an antitank battalion. The two tiny circles beneath the symbol signify wheels meaning the unit is motorized. Vehicle front registration plates measured 9x47.5cm and rear plates were 20x32cm, although the latter were often also used on a vehicle's front.

19 September 1939

Officers of XIX.Panzerkorps meet with soldiers of a Russian tank brigade near the city of Brest Litovsk. The Red Army had invaded eastern Poland on 17 September with seven armies, and due to the almost total lack of Polish resistance, Soviet cavalry and mechanized units were able to push forward with great speed. The Soviet tank crewman is leaning against what appears to be a T-26A light tank. The left arm protruding into the photograph from the left is unidentified, but may be SS-Verfügungstruppe as they did wear regimental titles on the left cuff. Few cuff titles were authorized by the Army at this time and those that were worn on the right cuff.

"Danzig grüßt seinen Führer!" (Danzig salutes its Leader!) proclaims the banner as Hitler's motorcade parades through the cheering crowds of liberated Danzig. Hitler, surrounded by bodyguards, is standing in his specially protected Mercedes-Benz 770 G4W31 touring car. His bodyguards were forced to keep close to his car to try and catch or deflect the many bouquets thrown to him from balconies and windows.

Hitler embraces a grateful Danziger. An SS-Stabsscharführer (equivalent to an Army Stabfeldwebel—staff field sergeant) of SS-Leibstandarte "Adolf Hitler" cautiously watches. This photograph was probably taken after Hitler's famous speech in the historic Guildhall, which was built in the 14th century during the peak of the Teutonic Knights' domination. Hitler left to tour Danzig Harbor where the first shots of the Second World War were fired against Poland, directed at the Westerplatte garrison, on 1 September by the old battleship Schleswig-Holstein.

20 September 1939

Decorating his men is General Ferdinand Catlos, Chief of Staff of the Slovak Army, decorates men of the three Slovak infantry divisions taking part in the invasion of Poland under the German 14.Armee. Although German officers looked upon Slovak troops during the campaign as a marginal military force, Hitler viewed their alliance as a very useful propaganda tool against the Poles and the world. The Slovakian uniforms were a light olive drab of a shade similar to the Polish uniform. Black, white, and red swastika armbands and their distinctive dome-shaped helmets helped to identify them as allied Axis troops.

Advanced elements from XXII.Panzerkorps had reached the city gates of Lwów as early as 12 September, but it was the 1.Gebirgs-Division of 12,000 men that was given the task of storming Lwów. Unable to force an entry into the well-defended city, over the next few days other units from 14.Armee were deployed to the city including XVIII and VIII.Armeekorps. They pressed a series of heavy assaults, but it was not until 20/21 September that the city finally capitulated. Here a Polish cavalry officer meets German officers to negotiate the surrender of the Lwów garrison.

21 September 1939

Thousands of Polish rifles have been captured at the end of the operations to eradicate the Kutno pocket on 19 September. Some 170,000 Polish prisoners of war including those soldiers captured in the Radom pocket by 10.Armee were rounded up. Two soldiers can be seen clearing Polish rifles to ensure they are not loaded. Since Polish rifles used the same 7.92mm cartridge as the German, many Polish rifles were later used by training and security units.

22 September 1939

On 20 September Hitler ordered the withdrawal of all German units east of the agreed demarcation line with the Red Army in order to minimize any conflict with advancing Soviet forces. Many German commanders were reluctant to pull back from ground won at great cost in German lives. To ease the withdrawal to the new frontier, which ran roughly along the four main river lines, German units fell back through a series of phase lines. Here a column of vehicles, led by a Horch staff car, withdraws through a town recently won in a bloody battle.

Life goes on…for now. An unconcerned farmer ploughs his field as a column of German tanks pass by, here a Pz.Kpfw.II and a Pz.Kpfw.IV. This had by now had become a common occurrence.

25 September 1939

A 3.Armee 10.5cm gun pounds Polish defenses of the town of Modlin with direct fire. The large trail spades seen on earlier photographs of German heavy artillery were detachable and if the ground was sufficiently firm need not be used. It was at Modlin that Panzerverband Kempf and SS-Standarte "Deutschland" executed a series of assaults against the strong Polish defenses, until they finally forced the enemy garrison to surrender. The investment of the Modlin fortifications lasted from 19 to 28 September. After the Polish campaign the artillery arm was criticized by senior commanders for not moving forward quickly enough to give continuing support to the attacking infantry.

26 September 1939

Pz.Kpfw.Is and IIs advance with infantry under artillery support further into Warsaw the day before its capitulation. Note the machine gun crew covering the route of advance.

These sequential photographs demonstrate the destruction of a main road leading into Warsaw just before the capital surrendered on 27 September. These soldiers are from 8.Armee, which had been ordered to accept nothing less than completely unconditional surrender. Within days of constant air and ground bombardment almost 140,000 Polish soldiers of the Warsaw Army laid down their arms, including some 16,000 wounded. Some 40,000 civilians had died, 10 percent of the buildings were destroyed and 40 percent damaged.

27 September 1939

Preparations to storm the Modlin fortifications by Panzerverband Kempf and SS-Standarte "Deutschland" were not completed until 22 September when patrols were sent out to determine enemy strength and probe weak spots in the defense. Under cover of Stuka and heavy artillery bombardment the pioneers of SS-Deutschland blew gaps in the barbed wire barriers and penetrated the position. The Polish garrison was finally forced to accept defeat on 28 September. Here an SS-Verfügungstruppe NCO inspects the foliage-covered pillbox at Modlin. Some of the camouflaging vegetation has been pulled away to reveal the firing embrasure. The firing port's stepped construction was designed to prevent bullets from ricocheting into the opening.

28 September 1939

Major General Tadeusz Kutrzeba (far right), Deputy Commander of Warsaw Army, with Major General Aleksander Praglowski, negotiate surrender terms of the capital with Colonel General Johann Blaskowitz, Commander of 8.Armee, at the Skoda Motor Works, a few kilometers outside of Warsaw.

Following nineteen days of vicious urban fighting the Poles finally surrendered Warsaw on 27 September. Here a white flag from a half-destroyed building symbolizes that defeat. An effort had been made to fortify this building by planking up the basement windows from which the defenders had fought with some protection from artillery and mortars. Some defenders would occupy the upper floors though.

29 September 1939

An officer from Panzerverband Kempf at Modlin interrogates blindfolded Polish soldiers. It had been units of II.Armeekorps that had besieged the near impregnable town of Modlin. However, with the fall of Warsaw large numbers of heavy artillery became free for transfer to the town and its massive fortifications. The intense artillery bombardment that began on 28 September was enough to convince its Polish commander that further resistance was futile.

A lieutenant inspects captured arms, equipment, and munitions that XVI.Armeekorps assembled in a town square. The wicker cases stacked opposite of the TKS tankette contain artillery rounds. The mounting bracket on the side of the TKS allowed the internal 7.92mm wz.25 machine gun to be externally mounted for antiaircraft defense. Below the wicker cases is an unusual little weapon, a 4.6cm wz.35 platoon direct-fire mortar.

2 October 1939

A 30.5cm (12-inch) Mörser (t) bombards the last pockets of resistance just north of Warsaw. This was an impounded Czechoslovak Skoda vz.16 mortar. The crew is withdrawing after loading the weapon. The Germans employed a number of heavy siege weapons, usually organized into batteries of two pieces. Up to two days were required to emplace one of these heavy pieces necessitating the digging of a substantial pit in which to emplace the bulky mounting platform and cradle.

5 October 1939

With the fate of Poland sealed, Hitler flew to Warsaw where a victory parade was held in honor for elements of the six divisions that had taken the city. For three hours, infantry, armor, cavalry, artillery, reconnaissance, pioneer, signal, and other troops marched past along the broad avenue from the Belvedere to the castle. Hitler is seen reviewing a drive-past of Pz.Kpfw.IIs, now cleaned up and sporting fresh painted Balkenkreuzen with which they had begun the campaign. The five long, brutal years German occupation had commenced.